SIGNATURE SOUND

Signature Sound

"WHAT DO YOU SOUND LIKE WHEN YOU SPEAK?"

Anthology: Volume 1

Signature Sound

Contents

First Printing, 2022

Introduction

We never truly know what will emerge when we first plant a seed.

We might have an idea, an inkling.

What sprouts is not only a result of the soil in which it was planted, but also the hands that cultivate it.

We dig in with our hands, taking with us remnants under our fingernails.

We water, then we wait.

A process that asks of us a great deal of faith, that our habitual toil will one day become the makings of a budding relationship.

This was a seed planted on route, a blossoming conversation volleying on piqued ears.

We were on the road to vision quest.

Four days and nights on a mountainside.

No food.

No phone.

No books, pens, or paper.

Alone with a sleeping bag and Mother Nature.

It's amazing how much you are able to hear when you remove the noise.

Signature Sound is the fruit born from an honouring of listening.

A deep reverence to an art lost amidst a sea of hollow words.

When we tune our ears in this way, we give ourselves the opportunity to hear unique voices that are buried beneath the mimicry.

This is a collection of songs that only these voices are capable of singing.

A harmonic response to being in rhythm and coherence with our own nature.

A fire inside.

Spirited.

Animate.

Alive.

1

AUM

Kristina Garla

Untitled

1

speak out loud
and petals find their creases
with the reflection of the
sun in the morning dew
stones form a smoothness
along the wind
and water too, while
rainbows breathe
their colours
speak out loud
and butterflies
whisper as a
cloud moves
a magpie
throws his
head back
to the sun
and sings
the beating
heart of
an army
of ants
echoes
within
when
we

speak
out
loud

2

speak out loud
and the washing machine
hums as the towels
roll around in the
water and soap
the bees buzz as
the dirt is moved
and plants are placed
in new warm homes
speak out loud
and birds chirp
serenading the
pegs as they
are clipped
onto clothes
washing
gloves
make a
squelching
sound as
plates are
scrubbed
the
vacuum

screams
the kitchen
fills
with the
kettle's
steam
when
we
speak
out
loud

3

speak out loud
and cracks form
in the earth with the
blood of babies
and women wailing
above the sounds of war
the air moves stones
thrown at the naked
flesh of a young girl
scorned
speak out loud
and toddlers
whisper as a
gunman moves
a mother
throws her

head back
to the sun,
and screams
the beating
hearts
of refugee
children
are but
broken
dreams
when
we
speak
out
loud

4

it is
the
silence
of a
barren
land
so, please
gently
speak
out
loud

Dr Emoto is coming for dinner

"You fool!"

He spat the words over his shoulder as he stormed out of the bedroom. She shrank a little as they reached her. Curling her toes. Her hands in tight fists. The sound of the front door closing hard echoed through the house. She heard him stomp down the path, muttering under his breath. Then there was silence, for just a second after he slammed the car door. The brief pause broken by music blaring, the engine revving, and tyres screeching down the street.

Slowly and carefully, she unfolded her body until she was sitting on the edge of the bed, her feet touching the cold unsympathetic floor. She sighed and with much effort, lifted herself to standing.

Savouring the stillness of the house, she made her way to the bathroom, undressed and turned the shower on. While she waited for the water to gather heat, she stood at the vanity, her hands resting on the edge of the porcelain sink. She leaned towards the mirror.

"You fool," she whispered. She watched her body twitch. "You fool," she said a little louder, again and again, until the steam made her disappear.

After showering she dressed and the physical pain of her body was almost unbearable. She swallowed her medication and managed to get to the kitchen where she sat for a while. Breathing. Waiting. Eventually her body settled, the drugs began to work and she could move again. She went about her usual routine slowly cleaning the house, making sure everything was just the way he liked it; things in their place.

She rested whenever needed. She rested often. Her tired bones sighed each time she collapsed into a chair.

After lunch she slept, desperately in need of recovery. She woke with tears running down her cheekbones and into her ears. With the palms of her hands, she gently smoothed the tears into her skin.

She spent the afternoon with the one plant he had allowed her to have inside. "You are beautiful," she said, caressing its leaves and lovingly watering it.

As the sun softened, she managed to make dinner. The effort completely depleted her. Regardless, she met him at the front door with a smile when he arrived home. "Hello," she said. He frowned and without looking at her, stormed passed. And although he did not touch her, she fell.

Gingerly, she picked herself up off the floor.

"I made dinner."

"I already ate."

The annoyance in his voice hung between them for a while.

“Oh,” she answered, trying to swallow her disappointment as it rose to her cheeks.

As he placed his jacket over the kitchen chair he looked around, paused and then said, “You are pathetic. Useless. You can’t even clean the house.”

They did not speak out loud for the rest of the night.

And so it went on like this. Each day, a slightly different rendition of the same song.

Then one day a small flower appeared on the plant she lovingly tended. The soft and bright petals filled her heart with joy. “You are beautiful,” she said gently, her voice lightly coloured with devotion. She felt something shift.

The next morning, while at the sink, before the steam dissolved her, she whispered, “You are beautiful.” Unexpectedly, this was followed by a brief and hesitant smile.

And so it went on like this. Each day, her smile slightly increased, lifting her heart and the corners of her eyes.

Over time her pain diminished. Her body straightened. She moved more freely. She astonished herself at being able to reach her arms above her head to do her hair. Something impossible for years. But he did not notice any of these changes. He just kept repeating, “You are pathetic. Useless. A fool.”

Then one night he came home and she did not greet him at the door as usual. He paused, confused. The air held the familiar aroma of dinner but there was also the delicate scent of anticipation.

"Hello?" he said.

Silence.

When he walked into the kitchen, she was sitting at the table, with the most radiant smile on her face. He stopped abruptly, unsure of what to make of this. The uncertainty shifted his sense of balance for a brief moment.

She picked up her plant and carried it, like a babe in the crook of her arm, as she walked towards him.

She daringly kissed him on the cheek. He smelt the sweet scent of her skin. His eyes softened.

"This is goodbye," she said with a gentle kindness, as she walked out the front door. "Oh, and Dr Emoto is coming for dinner."

He scratched at his chin, watching her silhouette as she disappeared, with her plant, into the night air.

And then, as he softly closed the door behind her, he whispered into the silence, "Goodbye beautiful."

Kristina Garla

Kristina Garla was born on Yorta Yorta land to Lithuanian refugees. Her favourite childhood memories are running on the hot riverbank sand and eating her Baba's homemade kalduny. Kristina has a special connection to where land meets water. She grew up spending a lot of time swimming in muddy creeks and rivers, beautifully clear bush streams, and the salty ocean.

Kristina has been writing from the body for as long as she remembers; allowing stories to come through her, writing from the salt on her skin and sharing what her bones know. She loves the art of slam poetry and spoken word as much as she loves to write. She believes something exquisitely changes within us and around us when we speak our writing.

She lives on Wurundjeri Country and her voice holds space for people to heal through meditation, somatic and grounding practices, and her published writing. Kristina is blessed with two beautiful children, who keep her humble. She collects feathers; and magpies tend to hang out with her when she meditates in her backyard. Their song brings a beautiful sense of harmony and joy to her heart.

Kristina peacefully insists for truth and believes in the guidance of love to change the world.

kristinagarla.com

2

Unearth

John Hartung

Jarring
A guinea fowl squawking
Begging to be hand fed

Bellowing
A threatened, territorial bear
Primed to defend

Squealing
A pig being brought to slaughter
Longing to roll in the mud

Only when things have gone on...
for too long, too fast, too hard.
When I'm cast adrift...

Not a dandelion seed dancing in the wind
But waterlogged deadwood alone
and battered about the waves of a torturous sea.

But is the deadwood really alone in the vast ocean?
And does the tempest really last?

Eventually...for awhile,
Or a brief moment...

The waves flatten and the waters calm,
the skies open and the sun peeks through.

What do I sound like then–
when there's nothing and no one to talk to?
Save for the fish and the birds and the skies and the sea.

The more I fall silent,
the more I can stay afloat
among the battering waves.
The more I fall silent,
the more I can row
in calm waters…

Towards the land
and the smoke,
and its' flames…

Toward the people
and their arrows and daggers,
or gifts of tropical fruit in hand-woven baskets.

I know what I'll sound like then.

I will speak with the archaic remembrance–
I am not only one with the sea but also the land.

Dense deadwood may sink,
but ships recovered from the oceans' depths
hide away long-lost treasures.

Everything takes shape, but all dissolves into formlessness. And from formlessness, everything takes shape. As God tells Adam in Genesis, "For dust you are and to dust you shall return."

Do I fear formlessness because there's nothing to cling onto? Do I sense risk in diving into the abyss?

But fear is preposterous. Fear is flinching from depth and death –averting one's gaze from the Muck and the Pure. Fear is the foundation of distraction.

Where do you want to go? I don't know.

What do you want to be? I don't know.

Why do you do the things you do? I don't know.

When will you decide? I don't know.

How will you go about things? I don't know.

I do not know.

I,
identity

do,
action

not,
negation

know,
awareness.

What does *I don't know* really mean? It means the ego thinks thoughts and performs actions unaware. Of course it does. Can one really expect the mind to *know*? The mind thinks *things.* The heart *knows.*

The mind is two. The heart is one.

The mind divides. The heart connects.

To be at war with oneself and others is to live in the mind. To believe the lie of separation. To split the world into two.

To be in union is to live in and through the heart.

Hiding from my reflection, I cling to my rigid shape. I say "I am this" and "I am that". In reality, I am "not this" and "not that".

I find security and comfort in clinging to a shapely form that fits into a neat, little box, but I must use my own hand to crank, crank, crank that box until the clown fully pops out. Refusal? Not an option. I've done that. I've seen the clown already. To find my true voice requires I continue to crank, revealing to myself the clownish caricature lurking in the manufactured box. There's no going back–no closing the lid and cramping myself inside, forever contracted.

Our predefined shapes are just for show. We don't consciously realize this. The clown purposely paints on the gaudy makeup and flamboyant dress. But if we think we are the clown, unaware of the makeup and the dress, we'll play out our programmed impressions over and over and over again.

I find my notion of shape often becomes too cornered, too obtuse. I find myself contained inside its edges.

But I am remaking my shape. I am assuming a new shape. Not once, but time and time again.

Not angular shape; rather, seamless shape, like the undulating form of an adobe abode in the arid desert 40 miles south of Albuquerque.

Seeing myself as a home not built, but grown out of the earth, as though shaped by Nature herself–walls formed of mud, straw, and grass, and smoothed by plaster to create a dwelling place for a soul, not seen separate, but seamless.

Energy-efficient. Sustainable. Durable. Healthy.

I am the axis mundi of my existence. Not of the world. Not of anyone else's existence. But my own. I stand at the center, and I may venture in any direction.

I may walk blindly directly into the thicket of thorny bushes and hope I'll pop out on the other side. And I will, eventually, but why wait?

Why not walk with my eyes and ears open, dancing around the cacti, scanning for venomous snakes?

When I seek beyond myself, I'm walking blindly into the path of my own destruction. I'm walking into a trap of my own creation, moving in ignorance, led by egoic accord.

True Accord is to walk with heart, mind merely the tool.

It can be called many things, but it cannot be defined. It cannot be conceived in the mind. It cannot be neatly contained, captured, or encapsulated. It cannot be sold, or bought. It cannot be taken away.

It can only be felt. It can only be recognized. The True Challenge is to coax it into form. To let it be realized.

Phantoms of the mind
Grifting
Drifting
Ever waltzing
In and out of frame
But always
There
Swirling
Spun up
Like a spinning top
On a long, round
Mahogany
Table
Rumbling
Time suspended
The spinning stops.
Past, power-hungry narrative circulated in my mind:
"I'm going to garner attention whether you like it or not!
I got a lust for power and a head full of pot!
This world's not alright; it is a sad sorry lot!
So give me the reins, I'm here to bust up the spot!"
Present, loving awareness springs up from the soul:
"Kickin' up dirt
I'm here to work
To burn away all that rot
That resides in the heart of the one who forgot..."

Dance between Form and Formlessness.
Balance is the Middle Way.
It is not convenient. It is not easy. It is not comfortable.
Are you getting it? Or do you still think you're you?

John Hartung

John is an attempting synthesiser of disparate ideas and paradigms. He finds inspiration in natural landscapes and the great outdoors. He lives for a good story and loves a good joke. A teeming mind finding his heart, John's on an undying search for greater depth.

The search led him to briefly living in different places: big sky country (Montana), Middle Earth (New Zealand), and The Land of the Sky (Asheville, North Carolina). But he's spent most of his life living in his hometown, Kansas City, where he's worked at various golf courses, studied history and literature in college, and performed stand up comedy at local bars and clubs. You can often find him geeking out about, and implementing principles from ancestral health and functional fitness.

John recently left his advertising profession to realise his dreams of building startups and pursuing entrepreneurship. He aims to expose fraud and advocate for a more humane and ethical digital advertising ecosystem. But he might end up finding himself moving into his RV and heading for the mountains and rivers. Time will tell.

3

Cancer

Justin Fox

In 2018 I found myself smoking an ounce of weed a week. I didn't talk to friends. I was comatose. I didn't sleep in my bed. I had a scab on the right side of my head that I picked off every day. I didn't shower. I collected big piles of dandruff and dead skin. I urinated in empty soft drink bottles because I was too lazy to walk to my own bathroom.

I hit rock bottom.
I couldn't find a reason to live.
I was over it.

Despite protest, my Mum dragged me to the doctors. It saved my life. I was diagnosed with bipolar 1 disorder and prescribed antidepressants. I had always been more of a *"rehab is for quitters!"* kinda guy. I believed that people who were dependent on antidepressants were weak.

I was scared of my Dad as a kid. His parents were hard on him and he was hard on me. He was a large, proud and strong Buddhist man, but I saw a profound transformation in him when I was 18. He was diagnosed with terminal cancer, and as it ate him alive he grew weaker and I took that weakness in a bad light.

* * *

It's foreign to him
Yet it eats away freely
It has no brain or body
But the face of death

* * *

In his dying days some random white-eyed priests at the hospital pressured him into converting to Christianity to secure his entry into heaven. He gave up the fight. Became a Christian. Then passed.

I was disappointed in him for giving up.

* * *

I don't feel sorrow
I feel hatred
Just like you, I have turned to GOD
But I blame him for everything
I use his name only in vain
And he relieves my sorrow

* * *

When he died I decided to inherit his strength and I vowed never to be weak. I gave myself a deadline. Dad passed away at 47, so I had until 47 to do absolutely everything. I was hungry. I was obsessed. I've been there. I've done that and then some. I'm now 47 and I believe that this self imposed deadline drove me to make the marks I've made to date, but it was only a few years ago that I learned the hard reality of not being able to choose when it all ends.

The meds helped me to avoid hitting low-lows, but they also robbed me from reaching high-highs.

I was in the middle.

I was numb.

Flatline.

Everything I had ever done of any worth in life had come from meeting the deadline and living through the death of my father, so getting off the meds became my priority and I'm happy to say that I've been clean for over 3 years now.

* * *

He hurts himself

Trying not to hurt himself

* * *

I've made peace with periodically losing my shit. I value the emotional connection I feel when I remember, somewhat romantically, my previous lows. I use my low-lows to create art.

I am an Artist.

If bipolar is about having inflated self-esteem or grandiosity, or being more talkative than usual, or distractible and an excessive involvement in activities that have high potential for painful consequences, then bring it! I choose to embrace these traits of my mental illness.

So to answer the question; what do I sound like when I speak?

Well, it depends which me you're speaking to!

Justin Fox

Justin Fox is a Visual Artist.

4

Envoiced

Austen Wigglesworth

Envisioned, Enlightened, Envoiced:
Speaking from the heart.

My voice varies based on who I speak to and why I am speaking. So does my writing. For a speech, the tone is different from sharing a post on social media. More than word choice or tone of written word, the voice with which I read it changes. Like vocal posture: just as I stand up straight for a formal occasion, my voice stands at varying degrees of formality depending on context. So too with my writing. Essays edited in the early morning; texts sent in the spur of the moment; stories adapted from myth and archetype; posts inspired by serendipitous beauty; poems in the dead of night: each flows with a unique tone.

Most of my writing for the last six months has been poetry. Here, though, it's hard for me to say whether my poems are good or not. Whether, in a vacuum, they reflect some glimmer of excellency. Poetry, like all arts, has some sort of standard. By which will I be judged?

Poetry also provides a freedom unavailable to other formats. A poem is sanctimoniously susceptible to impression and interpretation, each poem a request for participation, asking the reader to choose a frame of reference. I can read the same set of words looking for inspiration, and find it, or for an argument, and find that, too. I can focus on the rhythm and my experience is entirely different from reading with an eye for figurative language, even though it's the same poem.

Take this stanza for example:

There's a certain kind of sweetness
To letting a single sentence
Drip down the page
And take on,
As a result,
The succor of poetry,
Like onions caramelizing:
Simultaneously shrinking
In size
And expanding
In flavor.

Read from the page, the meaning of the stanza is emphasized in that it's doing what it's saying: a single sentence, broken by lines, is "dripping" down the page. This effect is as visual as it is literary. The same poem becomes different if read aloud: the line breaks flow together and the sentence becomes one. The visual effect is lost. It's neither good nor bad, but it is different. Poetry accommodates a varied life, and the essence of each poem becomes something new depending on context.

I write simply to write. I write because it feels better to cast the words from my head than cage them in it. When I keep the words in, they spiral around in an increasingly painful way, like water coming to boil in a closed pot. Writing releases the pressure.

Words open the lid to my mind. There are many avenues to perfection in language: structure, significant meaning, references, figures and flourishes, sincerity. A perfect phrase can be perfect for its quotability, something timeless and universal. It can be perfect for its resonance, perfect in this moment because it is this moment. Both of these point towards truthfulness:

Words are perfect when they are full of truth. Not necessarily factual, but truthful.

With the written word, I record a state of myself. With the spoken word, I express my state of being. Words are personal and inherently collaborative: only with another do they matter. We transmit and translate, crafting something together that is simultaneously immaterial and devastatingly real.

In the end, I don't really know what I sound like when I speak. It's always a collaboration between speaker and listener. How do I sound to you? I imagine it's different from how I sound to me. Even my own voice is recognizably different depending on *how* I'm listening to it. If I'm listening to a recording of myself, whether on an episode of my podcast, in a voice note, or in a video, I notice myself in different ways than when I'm actively speaking. I've found balance in the combination of listening to recordings of my voice, speaking without thinking about it, and actively listening to my voice while I speak.

In this balance, I am learning to recognize when I am speaking truthfully. Speaking from the heart has a different resonance, beyond sound: the resonance of heart, mind, and soul.

> "Trust thyself: every heart vibrates to that iron string. Accept the place the divine providence has found for you, the society of your contemporaries, the connection of events. Great men have always done so, and confided themselves childlike to the genius of their age, betraying their perception that the absolutely trustworthy was seated at their heart, working through their hands, predominating in all their being."
>
> **Ralph Waldo Emerson, 'Self Reliance'**

The note plucked from this iron string is the pulse of life. Find it, and you have found meaning. I find that I most effectively unveil the sound of my string by repetition in the crafts of writing and speaking.

Words have the capacity to be either full or devoid of meaning. We may infuse them with meaning–it is something felt, something moved. A finger plucking the iron string. When they are empty, though, this too is felt.

In the short span of a single conversation, or even within the confines of a single sentence, words oscillate between fullness and emptiness. In Robert Anton Wilson's *'Illuminatus Trilogy!'* central protagonist Hagbard Celine, moments before being kicked out of a courtroom, passionately decries:

> "Why can't we say shit is shit, instead of calling it excrement? Why do we never use language to convey meaning? Why must we always use it to conceal meaning? Why do we never speak from the heart? Why do we always speak words programmed into us, like robots?"

How can we learn to speak from the heart?

Do it often.

Speak often from the heart. Listen to others who do the same. Listen to your own words. Drop your pretences and speak to the living, breathing, feeling moment of *you*, just because it is alive, and so are you. Learn to distil the shit from the gold.

Speaking truthfully is magnificently powerful. And only by listening to my own voice have I discovered how to hear it.

"Writing Poetry for Instagram"
By Austen Wigglesworth,
August 1st, 2022
Writing poetry for Instagram

Seems like a silly choice:
My lines aren't broken as I'd like them to be,
The voice in your head reads them differently
From how I wrote them, would read them, or speak them aloud.

Reflecting now,
It seems like writing poetry at all is a silly choice,
For it is only when the poem is animated by a reader's voice
That it breathes true life.

Writing a poem down is only good insofar as to deliver it into the hands,
Then mouth, of a proper reader,
Who speaks it aloud,
Whether alone or in a crowd.

In fact, this idea was compelling enough for me to roll up the windows in my car,
Open my notes app, set the microphone,
And speak aloud as I let the
Algorithm type for me.

Speech-to-text, then text-to-speech,
First by a computer, then by me, or you;
Any functional human bio-computer will do.

Thank you Mr. Lilly for the phrase,
And metaprogramming instructions,
And, although my eyes are focused on the road,
I see from their corners that the phone is having trouble translating your name
And terms from my mouth to page.
I suppose that I, too, am having trouble with my words:
The trouble of translation,
In general, or text-to-thought,
Or thought to speech or action.

When poetry is involved with life, the poem itself is not alive.
Even in its most living state–being spoken and listened to–
It is not experience itself.
It is a fragment, a fraction, a pale reflection of life, lived.

So, I guess it doesn't really matter if it's for
Instagram,
My notebook,
My laptop,
My phone.

The only thing to hope for is to reflect an experience of life,
A shadow in poetic form,
Which catalyzes the birth of true life.

Austen Wigglesworth

Austen Wigglesworth is a wayward poet, seeking solace in the beauty of words.

5

Compost

Benny Wallington

Words, words, words.
All over the place, words.

Inside the mind words,
the thickest thicket of all wall papers.
Words insincerely serve, words.

Hanging back for fear of failure, words.
Like auditory compostable worms.
Yeah they're a real bunch of
Compostable worms!?!

'Worms are great though!'

Yeah I guess.
The worms, die too and become worm food.
And the words, die and become word food.
So the mind is just one biggest little worm farm?

When you don't tend,
mend,
or bend
the farm starts to stink.

A worm farm.
Where the worm family have their own fields filled with cows and horses and chickens and pigs.
And veggies as far as the eyes can see.

The fruit trees fruit immaculately
on the worm farm.

They're traditional worms,
their cloth that of the old country and they hold worm parties with neighbouring farms to share...
Words.

A sliding swap of D's for M's and back again.

These words are like worms and worms like words 'round they go, around again.

So when the worms escape the farm they make their way across the seas to lands far far away and become invasive you see.

They take their families, their dogs and even their seeds with them and setup worm colonies.
And sometimes these worms full of words can't speak the words of the worms in new lands, so try treaties.

But these worms they take over place without a care in the Worm.

'HA. Fuck!
Enough of that".
'Nah,a little more.'
'K.'

The worms steal oxygen from the others. They're not the words of the land but attempt to make them seem that way.

They find a way through their words and ways to dismiss the Kings and Queens of their new lands. These natives worms, them into the ground.

Now you might say 'hey, ho, that's where worms like to go.'

But you see, the further down you go, the less likely you can save your way.

No matter how much you speak up, shout down or scream bloody murder, nobody can hear you.

In time,
new colonies of worms cry for home and for lost relatives they never knew because their words behind the thickets are starting to protrude.
Intrude.
Like their lineage once did.

The words.
Again the fucking words.

'So when do we get to the good part in this story?'

'Hard to say son.'

'Hard to say,' says the 5th generation colonist Worm Farmer
living the good life to his ungrateful 6th generation Worm son.
And thus, planted the seed for Worm War Three.
The wordier called it Word War Three.
And the wordier still, said,

'And in the end there was the Word, and the word was with
Worm, and the Word was Worm.
He was with Worm in the end.
Through him all things were composted; without him nothing
was recycled that has been regenerated.
In him was death, and that death was the light of all Worms.

And unfortunately,
on this ride.
There are no
refunds.

But there is
a thorny light through the thicket.
'HEY! DON'T TRY AND WRAP THIS STORY IN A NEAT
BOW SIR OR
I WILL SHOOT YOU WITH THAT BOW.'

Benny Wallington

In a world screaming for your attention, you will find Benny sitting solemnly on Bundjalung Country. His ears honouring the wisdom earned by deep listening. Beneath his fingernails, local dirt. A reminder of his dedication to connecting to Country. From amongst the quiet, he'll sing you a question, stopping you in your tracks. A forever apprenticeship which hones Benny's skills as facilitator, coach, activist and writer. As co-conspirator of the #GetConnected movement with his partner Jacqueline, Benny is dedicated to deepening connection through dialogue and ritual.

He flows when editing prose. His delicate attention and sharp blade finding the essence of a Signature Sound, weaving threads together with cheek, poetics and a love of line breaks. Your words will never be the same once Benny has met them.

Bio written by Steve Brophy

6

Voice

Lara Foster

I got tingles when I started writing. Reading aloud what I wrote. The words coming, landing, thudding. A rap in my chest.

Knock, knock, knocking.

I wrote that? A tender voice would ask internally, unsure of the eloquent stylings.

Oh shit! I w r o t e that! Another tone answering.

Observation watching this filter of notes pinging my body in different ways.

> *This lands.*
> *Not quite here.*
> *Say more here.*

In Elementary I created the words and pictures for a book that would be laminated and added into the school library. The story depicted a scuba diver's explorations underwater in Hawaii discovering a chest filled with treasure. I felt so proud of that book! So proud that my book was in the library!

Then in middle school I wrote about my dad's friend Pedro Sauer vs. Lance "The Bull" Bachelor. I'd made Pedro the hero, got an A on the project, then mailed it to my dad in Utah with a note that said, "Please read this to Pedro."

> *I don't know if he ever did.*

What I do know is after my dad passed away I acquired all of his life possessions, relationships and intergenerational trauma. His life was packed and delivered to me inside three hard cold steel shipping containers.

Inside, full of boxes, I found a file folder with my hand typed story of Pedro and the note still attached.

He'd saved it.

It's funny thinking about what paths actually lead us to the centre of our hearts. We hear people say, "Do what you love," and "Love yourself".

But it's not really something we can "think" about. Rather it seems to be something that we are willing to "be" about. Moving through our days listening, internally asking, "Is heart here?"

Not so much with words, but with the way we attend to our lives, our daily functions, our commitments and interactions.

Searching for heart.

My heart broke when my dad passed away. I know he completed his life's purpose but that didn't make it hurt any less.

The only way through the pain was to sit in the middle of my broken heart and write about everything that had landed with a thud in my chest. Opening the door to those knocks. One by one. Learning how to dance through grief.

Body in overdrive, I'd get out of bed at 4am every morning, surging after yet another sleepless night.

To write.

After years of writing for no one but myself, I started to share some of this pain, confusion and curiosity through a blog, hoping in doing so the burden would not feel so heavy for me, or perhaps someone else.

I kept writing.

Later, I began working with a writing coach reading every single one of my broken-hearted words aloud to someone who listened.

I wrote some more.

And then, one day, the writing turned into something else entirely.

I'd get so nervous before any blog I posted out to the world. I would re-read it aloud to myself dozens of times.

The tingles kept arising. Messaging, *That's* the line.

When I sat with the sense it would drop low in my gut. Releasing the message flooding down toward the bottom of my feet.

I'd share it with the world then fret, "What if someone mistakes the meaning?"

Reading the piece again, allowing the same line as before, to land, soothing, calming...

Oh, there it is. This is good.

I'd acknowledge this sense fully then swiftly turn to walk away and let the piece breathe.

Somewhere in the space of all those really good lines, the ones that tingle from head to toe, they started multiplying.

There it is again!

A whole paragraph, dropping, walking in time, to an invisible beat. A cadence from an unheard melody coming closer.

The snare of curiosity reeling me in.
What is this sound? Can I hear it again?
This tone. This rhythm. This blending of body, mind, and spirit.
This one, two, three... let's make a me.
My soul. My heart. My innocent choice.
To love and to lose.

So I could sing the blues.
And return to this rhythm.
Sometimes in the kitchen
of my very own beating heart.
The one that used to be cracked apart.
Did it heal?
Did I become whole again?
No.
This is something different.
This is an emergence.
This is voice.

Lara Foster

Lara Foster is an author, coach and developer. Her debut juvenile fiction novel The Healing Gem of Arcadia released in October 2022. She is so grateful to the humans who have invited, joined, and held her amidst this arena of living alive.

Lara's gift of resonance becomes magnified when she turns that mirror toward others inviting them to a dance with revelation. These are the moments where her words take flight. Free to play and lay where they will. Mostly amidst the bellies of readers who will receive them.

She lives in the Pacific Northwest of the U.S. with her partner Gretchen and their Olde English Bulldogge Kona Rose.

LalasLifeGarden.com

7

Cerita

Willy Lizar

I sound like an awkward boy stuck between two worlds who never seems to run out of stories to tell. Some might find me inspiring or interesting, while others are of the opinion that I am too intense! What can I say, I cannot please everybody, though I did try. I tried very hard to please everybody for a good portion of my life. As a young boy, I loved to tell stories or *'cerita'* in the Indonesian language, Bahasa Indonesia.

"Cerita dong"
"Cerita dong..."
"Ayo Cerita Dong..."
My relatives used to ask me.
"Tell the story."
"Tell the story..."
"C'mon, tell the story..."

Si Tukang Cerita, a story teller, was a title I held amongst my relatives back then. I loved the spotlight when I told those stories and everything that came with it. I was a very energetic boy. One of those kids that couldn't sit still. I used to zoom from one side of the room to another, paying little attention to my surroundings. Consequently, I would often bang my head against various objects, mostly walls, resulting in bumps all over my head.

"Ayo, cerita dong... kenapa jadi begitu?"
My relatives would later ask me.
"C'mon , tell the story... What happened?"

I proceeded to recount the events leading up to the point when I hit my head. My relatives would often react with laughter followed by jokingly suggesting that I should wear a helmet at all times.

This was an innocent time.
Well before adolescence where all the stories stopped.
Silenced I became socially awkward.

As an immigrant, I felt insecure the moment I set foot on Australian soil. I just wanted to be accepted. Unfortunately, English was not my first language, so I could not help but be different and I hated that. I have vivid memories where my closest friends in high school would tease my pronunciation of particular words. For instance, I would pronounce 'begin' as *"biggins"*. They would mockingly ask me to repeat the word again and again, then they would mimic me shortly after. No matter how much I tried to correct myself, I would continue to say *"biggins"*. It may have seemed to be an innocent joke amongst friends, but I took it to heart. I was embarrassed. I thought I would win their approval by letting them have a laugh at my expense.

I was not always like this...

There were a series of stories which led me to become this way. Now, before I delve further, I must let you know that I am a history buff. In fact, my childhood dream was to become a historian. What I enjoy the most about history is the storytelling component, retracing the steps of one's journey in particular.

How did a person become who they are today? Breaking down the defining moments, line-by-line and in as much detail as possible. So to explain what I sound like when I speak? You must understand how I came to be who I am today. My *His-story.*

Genesis

I am an immigrant from a developing nation. I am not someone who came from money. My parents came from humble beginnings. My dad would often tell the story of his wedding day where he took my mum home on the back of his scooter after the reception. It was a simple house without any electricity. Their house was a mere 3m x 11m, about the size of a studio apartment. Due to the poor sewerage system, my parents would often wake up to a flood of knee-deep turd water through the house. As you can imagine, not the best living conditions to raise a family.

Nevertheless, they were determined to have a family and so they raised four healthy boys as they hustled through various jobs. From a career as a parcel courier, to hiring taxis, then selling children's swim-wear until saving enough money to buy and sell second-hand cars, later transitioning to property. Basically anything they could get their hands on to generate income and put food on the table. Though, my dad always considered himself unlucky that he never had the opportunity to complete a tertiary education and be in a position to have a prestigious career. This is because, for a brief period before all the hustling, he had an opportunity to study abroad.

My dad arrived in Singapore to fulfil this dream but fate would have other plans. After just 1 month, he heard news about his father's deteriorating health. Medical attention was not cheap back then. To give you an idea, one blood transfusion procedure would equate to the price of a car. As the good son that he was, he made a conscious decision to return home unannounced to be with his family during his father's final moments. To support his family financially, he chose to join the workforce instead of returning to school, being the bread-winner alongside his now-widowed mother. His first job was to deliver his mother's freshly cooked meals to a bathhouse which was predominantly occupied by sex workers. The back and forth journey used to take him 4 hours, one he used to complete on a daily basis. I can only imagine the difficulty he must have gone through as an innocent young man straight out of school, just 20 years of age at the time. That is my family's history, the genesis of my story.

I was born in Indonesia where English was not commonly spoken back then. The national language of the country, Bahasa Indonesia, consists of different sets of grammatical rules, sentence structures and pronunciations. I did not speak or write in English until the age of 9 when I relocated to Australia. Naturally, I carried over some of the tendencies of Bahasa Indonesia into how I spoke English. Even after 25 years, there are still traces in the way I speak today! In the past, I would speak softly or refrain from speaking at all because I was afraid people would notice that I am different. Little did I know that these differences would make up my story. It is what forms the uniqueness to my sound and how I speak.

Hakka

If you are interested in ancient history, here's more. While I was born in Indonesia, my ancestors came from China. My Chinese ethnicity is *Hakka,* which means "guest families." The term itself bears historical significance as our ancestors migrated across China in order to avoid political unrest, leaving their native region in the north. Later on, my grandparents also migrated across the sea to Indonesia, chasing the promise of a better future for our family. Quite a fitting origin story and perhaps even foreshadowing my own fate.

Unlike my dad, I consider myself lucky. Due to an unfortunate — or fortunate, depending on how you look at it — turn of events, I was granted an opportunity to move to Australia. Indonesia is known for its long history of racial tension between the native of the land and its more recent permanent residents,the Chinese Indonesians — my people. While the exact reason for the tension is not known, I was told many horror stories as a boy that involved my parents and relatives being unfairly treated due to their ethnicity. For example, two of my biological brothers had to be adopted by my parents for legal reasons. This is because my grandparents came from China and were not allowed to become citizens. At the time, the Indonesian government would only issue birth certificates to newborns of Indonesian citizens. Luckily, my uncle had managed to acquire his citizenship prior to the birth of my brothers via the country's informal channel, bribery. My uncle then claimed to be the father of my brothers. He later transferred the rights to my dad through adoption.

Even during my years in Indonesia, I experienced discrimination quite regularly. For example, we were not allowed to openly speak, write or study any Chinese dialect. Anyone caught doing so would be heavily persecuted. My parents, however, saw the importance of preserving our cultural heritage and learning Chinese language was a way to do so. So they enrolled me into a school that secretly taught Mandarin. I did not know it at the time, but I was born under a dictator's regime. The idea of racism was too complex for a boy to fathom. I thought it was normal to follow rules. That our role as citizens was to do so rather than challenge or question them. That was the reality of our education system and my upbringing. Further, anyone with a Chinese sounding name would not be issued with a birth certificate or citizenship. That was how I ended up with the surname *'Lizar'* rather than a more common Chinese name like *"Li"* — a name I hated, by the way, as the other kids would mockingly call me 'Lizard' growing up.

History will inevitably repeat itself. That is certainly true for my family. Like my forefathers before me, I was forced to leave my country due to political unrest involving the fall of the dictatorial regime in 1998. As a last ditch attempt to save the regime, the country's dictator shifted the blame of the country's failed economy to the Chinese Indonesians who held important positions in the financial sector. As a history buff, I like to draw the comparison between the Chinese Indonesian and the Jewish during the Nazi Germany era in the 1930's, who were similarly used as scapegoats for the country's financial crisis. There were stories of violence all over the country fueled by racial motive: violence, robbery, rape, murder — you name it. At that point, my parents did what any good parents would do to protect their kids and sent me away to safety. Luckily for me, they always had plans for me to one day study in Australia — they had even secured our family permanent residency status. At the time, my brothers were already here studying. I suppose the turn of events only hastened this inevitability. This was my fate. My blessing and my curse. The price of safe passage to Australia was my voice, the one I had been using to tell my stories as a boy. I left Indonesia, jaded by the fact I was rejected by my own countrymen, unwanted by my birth country. I carried this with me as an adolescent through to adulthood as a sense of resentment.

F.O.B

I was often told as a boy that Australia was a lucky country. It was where I could get a good education and find a great job. That was how Australia was sold to me. While that is true, it is all a matter of perspective depending on how one defines 'good' and 'great.' Maybe that was true for my dad, who never had the education and career he desired. In reality, adjusting to Australia's way of life was not always smooth sailing for me. I resumed the remaining years of my primary school here. At first, I had a lot of trouble making friends and connecting with people, given I barely spoke any English. I made some friends here and there, mostly who were also non-English speaking. There were instances where I was teased for my ethnicity, but I was mostly bullied because of how I sounded when I spoke. There wasn't a term that described the mannerisms I carried back then, but these days it can be referred to as "F.O.B" — Fresh off the Boat. Each time I was picked-on, my voice grew softer and softer. Overtime, I became overly sensitive to how I presented myself to others. My self-confidence was shattered. I no longer enjoyed being in the spotlight. My stories were no longer worth telling and I just wanted to be invisible. I blamed my origin and identity as the source of the troubles I had in school. I was embarrassed and refused to admit where I came from.

Despite the lack of formal education, my dad is a wise man. He would often drop these truth bombs over dinner conversations, in the form of catch phrases which we were expected to adopt without question. One in particular is in relation to honouring our origin — *"Remember where you came from"* or *"blood is thicker than water"* he would often remind me, possibly as he saw how hard I tried to assimilate to this new environment I was living in. At this point, the thought of embracing my origin and culture was a sickening thought. Whenever he attempted to provide such a reminder, I was quick to reject his advice. I used to react with disinterest such as smacking my lips or even talking back on days where I felt like I had heard enough. Now, my dad is a lot of things, but patient is not one of them. He absolutely had no patience for talk-backs, particularly when they came from his son. Despite my intention to explain my position or convey my feelings about the hardships I was experiencing, he would hear none of it. That was the way we were taught in our household. Never talk back to your elders, especially your parents as they are older and wiser. Now that I think of it, it affected my ability to speak my truth confidently as I would be punished for it. So I started to keep things to myself whilst the sense of resentment towards my parents and upbringing continued to build. In my mind, their attempt to instil our cultural heritage was against my mission to become an *Aussie*, thus gaining the approval of my peers.

CC

Getting through primary school was challenging but high school was something else. Teenage life is complicated. There was no room for vulnerability, especially for a short-statured immigrant with a foreign accent. On top of my on-going insecurities with my cultural origin, I was also discovering my sexuality. Combined the two together, I had 6 years worth of agony, pentup sexual frustration and a low self-esteem. While I eventually found my crew in high school, who are still my best friends to this day, I spent the majority of high school fantasising about a particular girl. It was the first clue that I have an addictive personality. CC was her nickname amongst her friends. Despite wanting to express how I felt towards her, by this stage the damage was done. I had no confidence in my voice. I was convinced that I did not have any attractive qualities worth showing. I was more or less mute, quiet as a mouse. Valentine's day in year 9 was the one exception. I gathered the courage to give her a stuffed doll in front of the entire school. It was after our Computer Studies class where we were classmates and I gave her the doll just as we were packing our bags before the next class. I had planned to give the doll to her earlier, so I deliberately placed my bag next to hers, hoping no one else would notice that I made this overly cheesy gesture. As I presented her the doll, our faces turned red like ripe tomatoes as the sound of *"Awwww!"* could be heard from all who witnessed, essentially the entire school! Overwhelmed with shyness, we could not even look each other in the eyes. *"Thanks,"* she said softly and we both went our separate ways to our next classes. That was one of the best moments of my high school years. Unfortunately, the rest were a series of disappointments as I could not muster the same courage to follow this act of bravery, only tons of overthinking and procrastination. Not even the assistance of our teacher, who conveniently sat us together in class, could give me the strength to strike up a conversation with CC. I was way too worried about what others would think of me and too unsure of myself and my identity. Somehow I managed to convince myself that we were two very different people and things would never work out. She was not born in Asia, she did not have a funny accent like me and my parents would never approve of her as we were not from the same country of origin. Though, the funny thing was, she is Chinese. The same ancestral origin as mine. Nevertheless, what seemed like a bunch of excuses became some of the stories I tell myself everyday. It was this mentality that I carried over into my adult life.

Fast forward 10 years and I was 26 years old. By then, I had tons of failed romantic attempts and had yet to be in a serious relationship. By our society's standards, I was unwanted. In my mind, time was running out and I needed to do something about it. Then I met a woman that was older than me by a few years. Through the eyes of my parents and culture, that is an unfavourable trait but I was desperate and frustrated by my parents' expectations of me. I needed to experience 'love' before I 'expire.' Most of all, she appeared to be interested in me, the first time this ever happened to me. We also shared similar stories; immigrants residing in Australia from the age of 9 who eventually faced identity crises. Our frustration over who we were caused tension in our relationship with both of our parents. On this basis alone, I thought she was 'the one,' at least someone who was willing to accept me for who I was and could relate to the hardships I went through. I felt I was no longer alone. At first it was great. I was able to be a confident person once again. I showed her all my talents and took her on all the exciting adventures I got up to. By then I was an active rock climber and regular party goer, and she loved it. For once I felt 'cool' and sure of myself. In contrast to the soft voice I had been accustomed to, I made deliberate attempts to speak with an overly confident tone to mask my insecurities. I spoke with a great deal of certainty about various topics without really understanding or confirmation of the facts. To say it another way, I was a fraud.

After a while, some old friends came knocking on my door. Their names were Fear and Shame. Reality was calling me home and it was triggered by a series of comments made by my then-girlfriend who started calling out my grammatical errors and the funny way I spoke. She used to point out that I need to correct my pronunciation and use of grammar to avoid judgement from others. She then proceeded to nitpick every single error I made throughout our relationship which led to numerous heated arguments. Each argument felt like the end of the relationship. What I thought was the best thing that ever happened to me turned to poison. We endured three agonising years. For those years, I felt lost. I was powerless. I gave whatever power I had to the woman that I thought could save me from my own shame and insecurity. I thought I could trust her with my darkest secrets and I was free from judgement. It took me three years and countless mistakes to realise I had falsely convinced myself that she was 'the one.' I made an error of judgement. A simple self-admission was all I needed to free myself from the shackles, and at this point I was determined to confront the cause of my torment. I was ready to face my fears head on.

Gereja Ayam

It was the year 2019 when I finally made a decision to return to my home country Indonesia, about a year after breaking up with her. I was deepening my meditation practice and just attended a 10 day silent retreat, a life changing experience I will never forget. For once in my life, I stopped running from my problems and gave myself the space I needed to look at these issues dead in the eyes. What I saw was a possible future, my greatest fear. I saw myself as an old man on my deathbed alone in this world, without anyone loving me. I was unsuccessful in finding love. How can I find love when I did not think that I was enough for anyone, not even myself? I carried shame for most of my adult life. Pushed away my own identity and pretended to be someone else. I was not an Australian, nor did I accept my Asian origin. And no matter how much my accent had faded, a pseudo-Aussie accent I picked up during my years in university, deep inside I was still that Chinese-Indonesian boy who was forced to leave his country. It was the moment I decided that I needed to return home and experience the country as an adult.

Cathartic.

A word that perfectly summed up my journey back home. I felt there were greater forces at play with some of the encounters I had. For one, I met a father in Bali who found the motivation to get up everyday because he needed to provide a better future for his children. Regardless of his poor financial status, he never seemed to give up and was willing to take on whatever work he could find. I could not help but draw parallels with my dad and the sacrifices he made to provide my family a better future in Australia. It made me think of the years of anger I carried towards him for trying to force our culture onto me and how self-absorbed I was in my problems that I took him for granted. Without his efforts, I would not be where I am today.

I then traded stories and befriended an older native Indonesian man who was on the path of redemption to mend the sins of his past. He would do this through his devotion to his faith and acts of kindness to others, regardless of the hardships. The single act of friendship between a Chinese and native Indonesian itself was a powerful realisation in my eyes as it would not be possible 20 years ago due to the tension between the two ethnicities.

Further, he explained that the hardships he experienced were merely his way of giving back for what he owed from the past. That message resonated. I saw myself in him. Sure, I had experienced difficulty fitting in, but perhaps it was for a reason. Yes, I was bullied growing up and maybe that was unfair. However, what I discounted was my own actions, as I was far from perfect. What about the time I bullied others? A story I used to happily sweep under the carpet as if I was just an innocent bystander. The boy I bullied was a relatively new student, a native Indonesian kid just two years younger than me. Adam was his name. I still remember him quite well. Despite being younger, he was already taller than me and I hated that, maybe even jealous of him. He acted like any young boy should: innocent, energetic and friendly to all. Unlike me, being different did not seem to bother him. As we were both Indonesian, he saw me as a big brother. Rather than uniting as one, I chose to become a bully myself. Perhaps the fact he was a native Indonesia was a bonus for me. As if I saw it as a pay back for the years of oppression. Once while we were walking home from school, I told him to stop. I instructed him to count "1, 2, 3" for each step that he took. Usually he would rush home after school so his mother wouldn't worry. Though, demanding that he do this would of course delay his journey home. Nevertheless, an instruction from his big brother was to be followed. After all, that was what our culture taught us; listen to our elders without question. And that was exactly what the poor boy did, innocent and obedient as he was. While I thought it was an innocent prank at the time, his distressed mother subsequently approached and warned me to stay away from his son! My action harmed others. So how was I so different from those bullies that caused my suffering for all these years? I was just like them. I *was* them. Unfortunately, I have not kept in touch with Adam. Adam, if by some miracle you are reading this, I like to say:

"Maafkan semua kesalahanku."

Finally, I experienced a sense of harmony and peace in my last visit to my home country. I saw with my own eyes, people working together regardless of their religious beliefs or ancestral origin. Whether they were Chinese or Native Indonesian, there was a true sense of community. It was common to see people gather and present each other gifts, whatever they had to offer. I witnessed villagers at the foothills of a mountain on the island of Java helping to build the homes of their neighbours. Not too far from this village, there is a church dedicated to unite and celebrate our differences. It is called *'Gereja Ayam,'* meaning "Chicken Church" in Bahasa Indonesia. The building's structure closely resembles the head of a chicken, though the original inspiration was meant to be a dove symbolising peace, freedom and love for all. It is a place where anyone may meditate or pray under one roof, no matter the religion. Besides its religious purpose, It is said the original intention of the building was to rehabilitate children with addictions and mental illnesses, a fitting place to end my story. It was there where I was finally able to let go of the resentments I had held for the last 20 years of my life. At last I found unity in my voice.

The Boy, The Teen and The Man

What do I sound like when I speak today? Like when east meets west and everything in between. When I think of my unique sound, I think of the three significant personal transformations I went through meeting in this middle place. When I am in my flow, I would speak courageously for the fun of it without any care of judgement from others just like I did as a young boy. There are days when I would feel insecure and have trouble spitting out even just a few words as I care too damn much about what happens next, just like I was as a teenager. Or, I force out a false display of confidence, hoping no one will ever notice that I am terrified inside, just as I was in my adolescence looking for myself. Yet these facets form my unique sound that I embrace proudly as each tells a story about the journey I had been through to get to where I am today.

Willy Lizar

Originally born in Indonesia and Willy migrated to Australia at the age of 9. While he moved at an early age, the ties to his roots are strong. His family's values are the backbone to everything he does. Having gone through many ebbs and flows in his life meant he has plenty of stories to tell.

Willy's story encompasses overcoming the struggle from mundane aspects of life. From growing up, seeking approval from others, finding love then coming to terms through self-acceptance. He writes from the heart with openness and honesty as that was what he was taught as a young boy.

He is a digital content creator and you may find his YouTube Channel - Home Chef Willy, where he shares his story about connecting with people through breaking bread.

8

Meanderings

Leslie Lau

He drops down onto the office chair, riding the slight recoil as the hydraulic mechanism bears his weight. Swinging around to face the computer screen, he straightens his keyboard and palm rest, ensuring they are neatly aligned. Before putting down a freshly brewed cup of coffee, he adjusts his well-worn novelty coaster. Ah, symmetry, he thought to himself. An exquisite nutty perfume effused from the mug as the laptop sang its waking tune. 6:27am read in the bottom right corner of the monitor — time to start the day. Carefully sipping the near-scalding elixir, his taste buds accepted this invitation to dance, a delicious jig shaking off the remnants of slumber.

*He went through his booting ritual. Load music player. Open and maximise note taking application. Check personal and business emails. Open instant messenger. Mid-relegation of a small army of emails to the junk folder, one in particular caught his attention. Titled "***(no subject)***," it was sent from an email address that he did not recognise. Curiously yet cautiously, he opened it on the reading pane, the body of the message simply containing eight words:*

"What do you sound like when you speak?"

"Huh, interesting..." *he spoke aloud. The inquiry intrigued him. He leant back in the chair, feeling the ergonomic netting conform to his now-reclined posture. Swivelling ninety degrees to the right, now facing the window overlooking the street. Coffee mug cradled in his palms, he held it against his bottom lip and gently blew into the liquid gold (or brown) bringing to a sipping temperature. Rising steam began to fog his glasses as the question gradually took hold, the background of birdsong and thin rays of morning sun creeping between buildings lulling him into a soft state of daydream...*

It is when I speak that I sound least like myself. Every word I speak is something I've borrowed, not wholly my own. Each sentence, a product of mimicry. Like the lyrebird's song, my voice is often lost amidst the intermingling fray of countless others.

An explanation of sorts. Our physical bodies represent the threshold that separates inner and outer worlds. A border that is traced around the nation of "I." We cross this threshold each time we animate ourselves, both through our movements and how we carry ourselves. In the very same way, our mouths are the gates from where we release our oratory and auditory expressions. The final checkpoint before what was once ours is no longer. This is just one of many borders we need to cross, at each a fare we must pay.

It feels necessary to expand upon what I mean by the 'self' in this context. I am not who I say I am. I do not feel that I can be. Who I 'am' is simply not something I am capable of capturing with any spoken language. I also cannot be who I *think* I am, given our thoughts are formed predominantly through these same languages.

> "Words do not express thoughts very well. They always become a little different immediately after they are expressed. A little distorted. A little foolish."
>
> **Hermann Hesse, 'Siddhartha'**

Do I then feel who I am?

This seems a little warmer, though not definitive either. Perhaps we are most ourselves only moments before we exit our mother's womb. This may be the point where we could consider ourselves most whole, like a piece of fruit that has matured to the point of optimal ripeness. From this point thereafter, we are released from nature's nurture. In a very physical sense, the moment of birth is a threshold crossing. We exit the safety, comfort, and protection of one world and are immediately exposed to the influences of another. The umbilical cord is severed using surgical equipment. We are towelled down and stripped of any lingering purities. Mechanical instruments are implemented to stabilise and support our breathing. Each breath hereafter represents a distance placed between that original version of ourselves and the one that stares back at us through the mirror we gaze today. As the apple is plucked from the tree, it is cleaned, processed, packed, and transported into your local supermarket to be displayed under a sign in the produce section. The image of the apple hanging from its branch is a distant memory in contrast to the fruit you can see — but cannot touch — behind its plastic packaging.

How much of that original self is conveyed through the words we speak, I wonder?

Before I openly share my blunt views on world politics, a subtle force from within implores me to assess the readiness of the audience to receive, or I to shoulder any potential backlash. It is this internal force that reminds me, as mum and dad taught, to always greet and address my elders by appropriate method and title. It is what advises me to select words from a carefully-curated repository when speaking in a corporate setting. It urges me to use gentle conversation-ending tactics rather than plainly expressing my lack of enthusiasm for small talk. And the way that we navigate such situations is not limited to what we choose to say or not say. Donning a red trucker cap adorned with four letters, the depth and duration of one's bow, the up-rightness of one's posture, or one's wandering eyes can often say more than spoken words ever could.

These may merely be symptoms of growing up. As we mature, we naturally grow apart from this original essence of self. We are no longer who we were when we first entered this world. It is part of the literal maturation process both physically and mentally, the natural order of things. With each breath we create distance from who we once were before it. Akin to a flourishing plant, the greater it blooms, the farther it stands from the seed from which it emerged. Further, *where* we breathe also influences how we grow — a sprout will develop differently in a desert, a rainforest, and busy metropolis. It may be one of the first tastes of the environment that we get, its ubiquity representing an ever-presence of external influence in life.

Before a word is ever spoken, we are tasked to navigate through a gauntlet of competing narratives. The influence of our parents, family and loved ones. Our environment's geography and demography. Social and cultural ideals. Theological, philosophical, and political viewpoints. Our education, both formal and informal. Our each and every lived experience. Returning to the plant analogy, it is the water and nutrients we've absorbed so to stand as we do today. Inevitably, it all contributes to part of who we are in some way. We will feel each to differing degrees, see each from differing viewpoints, casting nuanced shades and textures upon this idea of 'self' that we each hold.

It begs the question, from where does our voice originate? How far does it have to travel before it is released into the big wide world? It is my sense that it arises from this original essence I spoke of earlier. The centre from which we came, the first semblance of self we may or may not wholly remember. This could very well represent our voice in its purest form. But it is no leisurely sojourn to the mouths cave. Our innocent little voices, heeding the call to be spoken, like a spritely Bilbo Baggins exclaiming, *"We're going on an adventure!"* as he skips over the grassy knoll. The journey is not dissimilar in epic proportion or its treacherous nature. It may only seem like a fraction of a second from a thought arising to it being vocalised, but we mustn't downplay the significance of what occurs in-between.

What are the branches that trip us up along the way? The dragons we must face and slay? All the things we have individually learned and now believe to be 'good' or 'bad,' 'right' or 'wrong,' 'yay' or 'nay,' will always act as a kind of filtration system between what we think and what we might say — these factors of external influence and conditioning as I mentioned before. Additionally, words have always been a limiting factor of expression for me. I've always struggled to find the right words to accurately convey what it is that I am thinking, feeling, or referring to on any given day.

> "Some things in life are too complicated to explain in any language...Not just to explain to others, but to explain to yourself. Force yourself to try to explain it, and you create lies."
>
> **Haruki Murakami, 'Colorless Tsukuru Tazaki and His Years of Pilgrimage'**

Amidst the throes of conversation, I feel this even moreso. Social etiquette establishes a general expectation around the timeliness of one's response in this setting. There is a fine line between thoughtful consideration and perceived rudeness — ignoring or not acknowledging what has been offered or said.

More often than not, in an effort to avoid an awkward interaction — another instance of conditioned action — I will choose a 'make-do' kind of response. For example, the question *"How are you?"* is so often a polite extension of a greeting that bridges into the body of a conversation. Simply responding *"Good!"* is almost the reflexive acknowledgement of this. There can be a real absence of sincerity from both sides in such hollow exchanges of words. As the recipient of this query, do I take it as what it is because it's what's generally accepted, in effect being dishonest as a result? Because it is an empty question, is it considered okay to return with an equally-empty response? What if the question is in fact sincere? Then it may be necessary to understand the substance of the question. From where is it being asked? Is it being asked generally or is it directed with specificity? Does the time between the question being asked previously matter? If so, what is appropriate to assume in terms of time periods? How about the relationship I hold with the one who asks? Does this also affect how I choose to respond? Should it?

Thinking about the response *"Good"* and what it might infer, an audible grunt may actually be more illuminating. However, this may simply form part of the unwritten rule set governing the social arena. It wouldn't necessarily be unreasonable to request a moment to deliberate, but again, how much time do we really buy ourselves? We already become impatient whilst awaiting a text response, watching as the 'responding' speech bubble intermittently appears and disappears. We can't exactly throw up the 'three dots' mid-conversation and ask for patience as we process our response. Although texting provides some leeway, we are still expected to respond within a timeframe considered to be 'reasonable,' else we risk our ears burning as our texting partner huffs and puffs in exasperation, wondering why we have yet to respond.

The effort necessary in writing what one thinks and feels cannot be understated. Words alone can never wholly represent our thoughts and emotions. In a way, we are using one language to describe another. This, inherently, could never be a completely accurate translation and will always fall short in some way. I would describe it as only our best efforts of internal interpretation.

> "Writing is in fact never anything but the poor and skimpy remains of the wonderful things each person has inside himself. What ends up as writing are erratic little clumps of ruins when compared to a complicated and splendid ensemble."
>
> **Roland Barthes**

The luxury we are afforded through writing, however, is time. There is a freedom to explore and inquire that speaking, for the most part, simply does not allow. There is a rapid fire nature in conversation. An entire exchange between multiple parties could conclude within the span of five minutes. When writing, it could take five minutes, five hours, or five days just to form a single sentence.

Within what is a fraction of time of translating one's thoughts and feelings into words, how could we possibly be aware of the myriad checkpoints we must necessarily cross? How could we recognise what we have sacrificed of ourselves along the way? And how could we discern between what is truly of our original essence and what is shaped by external factors? In that split second between thought, feeling and speech, an unseen expedition is had within. It takes a great deal of practice, but if we listen closely, we might be able to catch the tail of its echo. From here, we give ourselves an opportunity to consciously decide which words best-represent our unique sound. So when responding to the question, *"What do you sound like when you speak"*, perhaps this short meander might provide the slightest slither of a glimpse.

The fog slowly faded from his glasses lens as he gently rocked into attention from a recline, returning to a crisp view of the outside world waking through the window. Turning back to face the monitor, he is again confronted with those eight words,

"What do you sound like when you speak?"

6:29am flashed up in the bottom right corner, sending a tiny jolt of electricity through his body. With this, the last of his semi-dazed state was seemingly shaken away. Almost unconsciously, his hand hovered over the wireless mouse as if it had a mind of its own, he clicked 'delete' and sent the untitled email to the trash. Without a pause between, he returned to the unread inbox and continued scrolling...

Leslie Lau

Leslie is a humble Word Warrior.
'Smith' is way too 'white t-shirt' for his prose — plus, there's no way you'd catch him in white.
Sit with a Lau piece and it's like sipping a black tea steeped in the old way.
But wait! There are new leaves in the brew!
An honoured progression from the last, but never rushing to the next in this Lau lineage.
His writing is patient, cut from old bones and sometimes to the cliched dismay of the crowd, words don't do his words justice.
Heed the tide,
take the ride,
and embrace the guide that is Leslie Lau.

Bio written by Benny Wallington

9

Drift

Steve Brophy

***

His stare across the inlet of the mudflats meets an old Viking breeze. Brisk winds carrying tales of Valhalla amongst the Celtic songs. For a moment, his breath is stolen by the weight of the dreaming. Stolen by a sea of conquests and tragedy. Tear drops meet the lapping water at his feet as tribute to the blood spilled. Standing on the shore of Loch Gorman, the natural drift of the water keeps him mesmerised. Keeps him frozen at the water's edge.

The dreaming will do this, she tells him.

The dreaming will do this.

The edge has always cut him, but he can never steal himself away. The harsh realities of contrast spilling out along the seam where the parts meet. He finds himself here often. A fish out of water with legs to escape the world with, locked away by a cacophony of bladed words and disturbances.

Cowering to compress the contours of the shape he's long breathed in and out of, he knows today is different. A knowingness emanates from his bone marrow. Old wisdom uncovered when he steps out from behind an apology. Years of sensitivity and harsh reality have led this shape shifter to the edge of unknowing.

To the edge of amnesia.

Only the edge brought remembering.

Only the edge danced the dreaming back to his ear.

Only the edge brought her call.

As death beckons
there are but two paths.
To grip with futile might
or surrender to the
natural drift
of floating
out to sea

***

Being who you are, is what Joseph Campbell called, the privilege of a lifetime. She had not always lived into that privilege.

False prophets, naivety and the desire to be palatable steering her into more ditches than she'd like to admit. There sure was clumsy footing walking in the impressions of others. Standing with her toes gripping the cliff edge, she found comfort. A stillness. For years her father had screamed at her to step away from the face of death. But the edge kept on calling. Her father loved her dearly but his desire for societal palatability had long squashed her free spirit. He tried so hard to protect her from herself but in the end, he only drove her further away.

"Why can't you be like your cousin?"

Words of regret that would long haunt him. Words of love lost in translation.

She died with every attempt to save her from herself. Scars of desperate words covered her body shielding her from feeling anything but despair.

Why do we always hurt the ones we love the most?

But she knew today was different.

The faint whisperings of the dreaming had carried her here. Carried her to the highest point. To the place where the land meets the air. And the sea laps below in jealousy.

Standing at the edge, her fingers stroked her growing belly. Tears welled as she whispered to the life that would never be.

Cast your fear aside, dear one.
For you are imperfect
as you are
A feature, not a fault
Delight in your wonder,

your whimsy
your natural drift

***

Grow up they say.
Man up they say.
Death cries from slain souls screaming alive
the blade that cut them down
Be imperfect.
Drift out to sea,
with surrender as the winds
that carry you away
That carry you back
To the waters that held you first
To the life that dreams

Cue throat clear

Speak in full flight
Witness the majesty of silence
Dream alive the poetics.
Tease impossible apart,
Conjure the splendour demanded
to live with childlike exuberance.

Steve Brophy

Steve's words land close to the heart, because they have travelled from afar. A husband, a father, a brother, a son, a friend, a mentor, a teacher, a student. A master and student of poetry whose roots draw from fertile soils of The Emerald Isle. His wordplay is a weaving of vibrant and mythic tapestries. A lyrical dance of language sung through bardic blood. An elegant flutter of verse delicately emergent from the cocoon. A richness of prose drawing from the deep wells of a beautifully mosaic life. Put on a pot of your favourite brew, sit back, lean in, and allow Steve's rhythmic cadence to arrest your attention.

Bio written by Leslie Lau

The Journey

The Signature Sound Anthology is the artistic creation of our writing community that we call 'Reverberations.'

Reverberations is a place where writers come to find their voice. A journey from the offering of an inquiry to the publishing in print form. In this time together, contributors will have the opportunity to speak their work into life, an allocated writing companion to support along the way, three tiers of editing advice from a number of published authors, and more.

Whether you're a writer or an avid reader, we invite you to explore your creativity and hone your skills here in our writing community. If you'd like to find out more, visit our website below.

www.signaturesound.org

***

An Ode to the Journey

"Benny, Steve and Les. This spilled out of me this morning. A thank you to the three of you. It is raw and rough, there is so much more to come but this is what I have for you in this breath."

Kristina Garla

You have awakened her.

You have
awakened her
with your ideas,
your coming together
your Signature
Sound.

You have
awakened her
with your prompt
to ponder
what it means
to speak out
loud.

Her bones
opened their
eyes.

They stretched
and yawned,
delighted with
surprise.

You have
awakened her
and hearts sing
an abundance of
grateful.

You have
awakened her
and she flies high
as the words
tumble.

You have
awakened her.

www.ingramcontent.com/pod-product-compliance
Lightning Source LLC
Chambersburg PA
CBHW030416120726
47904CB00007B/2301

* 9 7 8 0 6 4 5 4 2 7 0 2 8 *